Original title:
The Sea's Quiet Song

Copyright © 2025 Creative Arts Management OÜ
All rights reserved.

Author: Isaac Ravenscroft
ISBN HARDBACK: 978-1-80587-417-1
ISBN PAPERBACK: 978-1-80587-887-2

Time Suspended in Brine

Waves tickle toes on the sand,
Seagulls dance, a raucous band.
Crabs host races on the shore,
Shells gossip secrets it must ignore.

A fish flips out, makes a splash,
The sun reflects, a golden flash.
A dolphin winks, spills the tea,
Then swims away, so carefree!

Seaweed flirts with bubbles bright,
While starfish dangle, quite a sight.
Dune bunnies hop and they play,
Under twilight's soft ballet.

Harmony of Ocean's Gaze

Fish in tuxedos swim with grace,
Crabs do the cha-cha, keep the pace.
Jellyfish glide, a silken show,
While clams hide pearls, their closet glow.

Splashing laughter in the swell,
Seashells chime a funny bell.
Mermaids giggle, each a tease,
Trading jokes with bobbing breeze.

Oysters bluff with stories grand,
Of hiding treasures in the sand.
The tide rolls in, a playful tease,
As fishes join in ocean's wheeze.

Dreamscapes in Endless Blue

Clouds make shapes of whimsical beasts,
While sea turtles host grand feasts.
Octopus juggles, quite a show,
To the rhythm of waves that flow.

Witty whales hum silly tunes,
Belly laughs echo with the moons.
Barnacles play hide and seek,
While sand dollars play truth or bleak.

The tides pull pranks without a care,
As crabby crabs steal sun hats rare.
A boat with ducks starts to sway,
Riding the waves, on a silly day.

A Song of Pearls and Shells

There once lived a clam in a cozy old shell,
He'd tell all the crabs they should dance at the swell.
With pearls in his ties, he'd boast and he'd brag,
But at tickle of seaweed, he'd shriek and he'd sag.

A fish fluffed his scales with a sweet little sway,
But tripped on a starfish that blocked his grand way.
The octopus laughed, oh, what a silly sight,
As they danced through the bubbles by day and by night.

Glistening Lies Beneath

A dolphin once claimed he could fly through the air,
But he flopped on the waves with a clumsy flair.
He swerved in his stories, the seaweed laughed loud,
While turtles just rolled, feeling smug and quite proud.

The pearls whispered secrets, oh, what a grand tale!
Of treasure troves hiding where sea cucumbers sail.
But alas, when they searched, all they found was a shoe,
Turns out the bold pearls were just joking, who knew?

The Stillness of Endless Waters

Anemones chuckled at fish passing by,
As they wiggled and jiggled, oh my, oh my!
A crab in a tux made a scene on the floor,
But tripped on his claws, rolling back for an encore.

The sea cucumber sighed, 'Please keep it down,
I'm trying to nap, don't disturb my clown crown.'
Yet laughter erupted, a ripple of glee,
As the creatures agreed it's life's silliness spree.

Notes from the Undersea

A pufferfish puffed up, oh what a bold scheme,
He tried to impress with a bubble-filled dream.
But with one little poke, he shrank to a dot,
All the fish just snickered, 'What a funny spot!'

A snapper named Sam, with a snappy little grin,
Said, 'Why catch some dinner? Let's just let it swim in!'
The seabed erupted with chuckles and glee,
As they realized life's better with a splash of folly.

Ballad of the Open Horizon

The waves wear hats of frothy white,
They dance and twirl in morning light.
A fish wears shades, feeling so cool,
While crabs play cards, breaking the rule.

The gulls hold meetings, take flight with glee,
Chasing their dreams, as free as can be.
A dolphin joins in with a splashy cheer,
While starfish gossip, hoping to steer.

Twilight's Gentle Tide

As day folds in, the sea grins wide,
A sunken treasure left to glide.
The sand's a stage for tiny feet,
Where shells applaud and crabs retreat.

The twilight whispers silly rhymes,
With playful waves, it counts the times.
A seaweed hat on a playful dog,
As jellyfish dance like a funky fog.

The Ocean's Embrace

With a belly flop, the penguins leap,
Into the blue, where secrets sleep.
They giggle and glide, looking so sly,
'Is that a boat, or just a pie?'.

The octopus throws a wild party,
Inviting fish—oh, how they all hearty!
With bubbling drinks and seaweed snacks,
They dance 'til dawn, no time to relax.

Hushed Currents and Gentle Breezes

Whispers breeze through the gentle swell,
The barnacles're planning their happy shell.
The tide rolls in with a playful shout,
'Watch your hats as I spin about!'.

The moon giggles at the cheeky stars,
As jellybeans float on candy bars.
With waves that chuckle, the night is bright,
In this wacky world, everything's right.

Secrets of the Deep Blue

Fish wear tuxedos, how dapper they swim,
Octopuses juggling, they're never quite dim.
With bubbles of laughter, the crabs dance around,
In a seaweed disco, they party profound.

Underwater giggles, the dolphins do share,
Whales tell great stories, if you stop and stare.
Glimmers of shrimp in a conga line sway,
The deep blue is filled with a jazzy ballet.

Cradle of Nautical Peace

Sea turtles float lazily, dreaming of cheese,
While seagulls complain, 'This breeze needs a tease!'
Barnacles gossip on rocks, quite a sight,
"Is that a clam's shell? Oh, it's just a kite!"

Crabs in a clam bake, all dressed up in style,
They argue on etiquette, stay awhile.
Starfish in top hats, such fanciful dress,
In the cradle of calm, it's a nautical mess.

Rhythms of the Rolling Surf

Waves play the drums with a splash and a pop,
Seashells are maracas, they shake till they drop.
A fish in a tutu takes center stage,
While jellyfish twirl in a dance of the age.

Sandy toes tap to the rhythm so slick,
The tide hums a tune, it's a sea shanty trick.
Whistles from gulls and a tidal ballet,
In the rolling waves, funny antics display.

Murmurs of the Coastal Wind

The coastal wind chuckles, blowing with glee,
It ruffles your hair, says, 'Now come, dance with me!'
Driftwood plays fiddles, the sand plays the bass,
As the breeze makes faces, it's quite the show place.

Palm trees lean closer, they're craving a chat,
While the sun gives a wink, wearing shades like a cat.
A beach ball rolls past, and the giggles ensue,
In whispers of wind, oh what fun we pursue!

Echoes Beneath the Surface

Waves are laughing, splashing bright,
A fish in glasses takes to flight.
Starfish hold a dance-off there,
With crabs who twirl without a care.

Giant clams in matching coats,
Sway as they sing with silly notes.
A dolphin's flip, a seagull's squawk,
Makes everyone forget to walk.

An octopus in polka dots,
Plays hopscotch on the sandy lots.
Jellyfish in tutus spin,
Underwater party, let's begin!

Turtles slide on seaweed slopes,
While mermaids float with crazy hopes.
The rhythm shifts, a bubbly tune,
In flash of fins, they dance till noon.

Melodies of Ocean's Heart

The bubbles rise and tickle feet,
As shrimp retreat in rhythmic beat.
Crabs don hats, they strut and prance,
Underwater, it's a silly dance.

Seashells drum with every wave,
Anemones, the kooky brave.
Barnacles sing with glee so loud,
While fishes form a wiggly crowd.

A whale hums jokes with every breath,
Echoing laughter, not of death.
The pelicans crack silly puns,
As laughter bounces, oh what fun!

With currents swaying, all around,
Jellybeans of color abound.
The coastal choir finds its song,
In watery realms where all belong.

Secrets Carried by Currents

What swirls beneath the ocean's face,
Are sea cucumbers in a race.
They giggle as they glide on by,
With seaweed crowns that touch the sky.

A turtle tells of tales so grand,
Of treasure maps and beachy sand.
Clownfish performing stand-up bits,
Drawing laughter with their witty skits.

The starfish wave with many arms,
In playful circles, sharing charms.
With every splash, a giggle flows,
In currents where absurdity glows.

From kelp to depths where secrets bloom,
Matters of humor fill the room.
In bubbles, tales ride as they swirl,
The ocean's laughter sets a whirl.

A Chorus of Shells

A conch sings high, a bivalve hums,
While clams compete as drums go thums.
Each shell a note in ocean's tune,
In sandy bars, they dance till noon.

A hermit crab dons quite a hat,
With shimmery shells, imagine that!
Silly stories swirl with each tide,
As marine life laughs and takes a stride.

The sea urchins write their own play,
With costumes made of seashells, yay!
As fish hold mics, they sing along,
Creating waves in laughter's song.

In shallows where the giggles rise,
The playful sea shares sweet surprise.
From basking sharks to tiny shrimp,
Each finds a voice in oceans' limps.

Stillness in the Blue

Waves giggle quietly, splashing about,
A fish in a tuxedo, feeling so sprout.
Seagulls are gossiping, stealing our fries,
While crabs hold a meeting, debating the skies.

A starfish plays chess with a floating bouquet,
Coconuts serenade the end of the day.
Shells bring the gossip, the ocean's delight,
As barnacles giggle at the moon's soft light.

Music of Distant Horizons

Tides play the trumpet, a jazzy refrain,
While dolphins do tap dance, showing no pain.
The whispers of waves are a comical tune,
Tickling the sand in the warmth of the moon.

A clam starts a band, with a jellyfish beat,
While turtles in bowties glide through their feat.
Octopus conductors flail their eight arms,
As seaweed sways back, with its quirky charms.

The Calm Before the Storm

In the still of the water, a fish makes a face,
And a crab does the twist in a clumsy embrace.
Sailboats are snoozing, their sails softly snore,
While a storm-cloud chuckles, 'There's fun in store!'

The breeze starts to chatter, exchanging some jokes,
As raindrops prepare to join in with the hoax.
The thunder, it giggles, a belly laugh loud,
Preparing to mingle with the darkening crowd.

Dreams Cradled by Water

Mermaids are napping, dreaming of fries,
While fish tell tall tales about big, giant pies.
A crab dreams of dancing, in shoes made of foam,
As jellyfish waltz in their glittering home.

The whispering waves carry secrets they know,
Like turtles who wonder where lost treasures go.
As the stars twinkle softly, a lullaby sings,
In the cradle of water, where laughter still swings.

Beneath the Stars

Beneath the stars we dance and twirl,
With crabs joining in, they give a whirl.
Seagulls laugh, as they swoop and dive,
Who knew that night could feel so alive?

A jellyfish winks, playing peek-a-boo,
While starfish perform a ballet for two.
The moon is a spotlight, glowing so bright,
As we giggle and glide through the shimmering night.

Water Cries

The surf pulls back with a comic sigh,
Like a dramatic child, it wails and cries.
'Hey, bring me back!' it shouts with glee,
As sand tickles toes like a mischievous flea.

It splashes around, full of playful charm,
Making everyone laugh with its playful harm.
A dolphin drums up a wavey applause,
As the humor in tides earns laughter's cause.

Reflections on a Calm Horizon

The water's a mirror, showing much flair,
But wait! A fish swims by, with a zoom and a flare.
It pouts at its reflection, adjusts with a shake,
Claiming, 'I'm handsome, make no mistake!'

Clouds drift by like cotton candy fluff,
As seagulls debate if this day is tough.
They caw about fish with a gossipy tone,
Who needs the gossip when you've got a bone?

Gentle Caress of the Foam

The foam rolls in like a friendly dog,
Trying to hug every leg, back, and smog.
It whispers sweet nothings, tickles your feet,
While singing a jingle most unrepeatable beat.

With every wave's crash, splashes abound,
It's a playful invasion, but who's gonna drown?
A crab scuttles off like it's late for a date,
While a turtle gives side-eye, knows it's too late.

Murmurs of Salt and Sand

Salt and sand engage in a whispering game,
Saying, 'Look at that kid, isn't he lame?'
They giggle at flip-flops lost in the fray,
As seaweed takes bets on who'll tumble away.

A hermit crab dons a new shell so chic,
Strutting its stuff like a fashion week freak.
Laughter erupts from the tides and the shore,
In this comic saga, who could want more?

Murmurs from the Tidal Edge

Waves that giggle as they crash,
A crab dances, all in a flash.
Seagulls squawk with a hint of glee,
While jellyfish jiggle, oh so free.

Sandcastles with frosting on top,
A dog buries treasure, a lollipop.
Buckets and shovels in a race,
The sun smiles down upon each face.

Flip-flops squeak with joyful cheer,
Beach balls bounce, far and near.
Tanned beachgoers with silly hats,
Waving to seagulls, trading spats.

As the tide pulls back, it laughs,
Changing fortunes like silly gaffs.
And as the day starts to retire,
The shore hums softly, never tire.

Nautical Reverie

Fish in their suits swim by with style,
Winking at sailors with a silly smile.
A parrot squawks with gossip in tow,
While octopuses dance, putting on a show.

Bubbles rise up, a charming affair,
While jellybean boats drift without care.
Pirate hats made of sewn-up seaweed,
Swap tales of treasure, no one takes heed.

Mermaids giggle, tossing a shell,
With every splash, a story to tell.
The sun dips low, it's time for a brew,
With nautical nonsense for a laugh or two.

As tides dance, pulling tricks unseen,
Laughter echoes in waters so serene.
Here in the harbor of whimsy and jest,
We find joy where the waves are at rest.

Songs of Resting Waters

Waves whisper secrets in a soft embrace,
Fish don tuxedos, strutting with grace.
A starfish grins, oh what a sight,
Making a splash with pure delight.

Seashells hold tales of laughter and jest,
With crabs wearing hats, they look their best.
Paddleboards glide like dreams taking flight,
Every splash seems to echo delight.

Sun-kissed cheeks and ice creams spill,
Ice-cream flavors that thrill and fulfill.
Seagulls perform their comical flight,
As dusk settles in, painting the night.

With each wave, a giggle is heard,
A tale from the tides, in rhythm and word.
Soft melodies float on the breeze's array,
Where waters laugh and frolic all day.

Voices in the Coastal Breeze

A lighthouse winks, keeping the beat,
While crabs roll around on tiny feet.
Seagulls dropping snacks in return from the sky,
Who knew dinner could be such a sly pie?

Kids chase the waves, then run back again,
Squealing and splashing like a wild hen.
Buckets and spades in a merry dance,
Playing in sand, giving joy a chance.

The sunset dips like a grand finale,
With dancing shadows starting a rally.
Mermaids giggle, their tails a splash,
As waves tickle toes in a frothy dash.

The coastal breeze hums a cheerful tune,
Bringing laughter beneath the bright moon.
Listen closely and you might just hear,
The nautical whispers that draw us near.

Chords of Horizon's Breath

Waves dance like a jolly clown,
Tickling toes in a sandy gown.
They whisper tales of fishy cheer,
While gulls squawk jokes for all to hear.

The sun wears shades, it's quite a sight,
As crabs do the cha-cha' in daylight.
Seashells giggle with a twisty grin,
Making sandcastles where fun begins.

Mermaids toss their hair with flair,
While dolphins leap, we've tales to share.
Tidal laughter fills the air,
As starfish clap in joyful flair.

Oh, the ocean's got a sense of glee,
With every splash, it sings for free.
So come and ride the playful waves,
For giggles found here are like hidden caves.

Petals of the Salt Wind

Whispers of wind make us chuckle bright,
As salty breezes sing through the night.
Crabs in tuxedos, oh what a scene,
They waltz in the surf; it's quite the routine!

A clam joked with a snail so slow,
"Why rush, my friend? Just enjoy the flow!"
While seagulls practice their stand-up roles,
Each joke they tell is full of holes.

Starfish lounging on a sunny rock,
Debate with seashells, who's ticked off the clock?
The ocean giggles, it bubbles and swells,
Telling all creatures the best of its tales.

The horizon bows, takes a gracious bow,
To each ripple, every breeze it allows.
With laughter so salty, we'll stay awhile,
In an ocean of fun, let's kick back and smile.

Twilight's Embrace on the Lagoon

Under the moon, the water does wink,
Fish gather 'round, they laugh and think.
The crickets chirp a silly tune,
While frogs jump high and sing to the moon.

A plump pelican balances a snack,
While herons jest, it's a feast, no lack.
The stars peek down with twinkling eyes,
As sea turtles pull off a wacky surprise.

Ripples of giggles float on by,
With laughter echoing under the sky.
Each sunset holds a comedic glance,
As the ocean sways in a merry dance.

So grab a shell, listen close, my friend,
For these whispers of joy will never end.
With twilight's glow and humor so right,
The lagoon's embrace is pure delight.

The Undercurrent of Dreams

Beneath the waves, a giggle stirs,
Bubble fish whisper silly blurs.
A starfish wearing a tiny hat,
Jokes with a clam, oh imagine that!

Seahorses prance to a tune in the deep,
While jellyfish giggle, their rhythm a leap.
Eels crack wise, their puns always slippery,
As anemones sway, looking quite chipper-y.

Coral reefs tell tales of underwater stars,
Mermaids laugh as they drive their cars.
Shells spin around, like dancers on cue,
Making the current a hilarious view.

So dive in and soak up this frothy spree,
For the ocean's humor is wild and free.
With every splash, find a chuckle or two,
In this dream of delight that welcomes you.

Whispers of the Tides

The waves chat loudly, full of cheer,
Crabs tell jokes that only they hear.
Fishy laughter bubbles up high,
As seaweed dances, oh my, oh my!

Seagulls squawk with humor divine,
While dolphins play tag, feeling just fine.
A starfish grins with its arm wide,
Who knew the ocean had such pride?

Octopuses painting with glee,
Their art makes the corals feel free.
A clam bursts forth with a joke so witty,
Even the barnacles laugh, feeling pretty!

Underwater puns flow like the tide,
Where every creature wears a broad smile.
No need for silence in this blue retreat,
For mischief and joy make life so sweet!

Melodies Beneath the Waves

Turtles strum shells, a band so grand,
While shrimp tap dance on the soft sand.
The echoing gurgles, a comical beat,
As the anemones sway on their feet.

Jellyfish glow with a disco delight,
Bouncing around, bringing such light.
A pufferfish opens, and what a sight,
It's not about scares, but a chuckle, alright!

Undersea parties, all around,
Where sardines spin, never to drown.
With laughter aplenty and games to play,
In this hidden world, fun finds its way!

The ocean hums to a quirky tune,
As crabs wield tambourines like raccoons.
With every ripple, a giggling sigh,
Beneath the waves, joy floats up high!

Lullaby of the Ocean Depths

Softly the currents whisper and tease,
At bedtime, fish share tales from the seas.
A clownfish jokes about its bright stripes,
While angelfish giggle at silly gripes.

The sea cucumber tells tales so bold,
Of treasure maps and pirates of old.
A sleepy stingray coasts with grace,
In this calm abyss, all find their place.

Starfish yawn, tired, though never blue,
Dreaming of donuts in the ocean's dew.
Crabby creatures snore with delight,
In this lullaby land, it feels just right!

Sleepy waves hum their watery tune,
As a light show glimmers under the moon.
And while the world rests in a gentle sway,
The ocean rocks dreams until the new day.

Serenade of Saltwater Dreams

Bubbles rise, tickling my nose,
As seahorses prance in cute little clothes.
Their serenade flows like a charming stream,
Giggling fish float, living the dream.

Sea urchins roll, life's very own wheels,
Joining the chorus with flapping fish squeals.
Even the whales join in, what a show!
Deep down, laughter continues to flow.

With every wave crashing, jokes collide,
When crabs crack puns, they never hide.
An octopus winks, sharing a laugh,
As clams giggle softly over their half.

Through dark waters, a light shows the way,
With every chuckle, time dances away.
In saltwater dreams, bright spirits soar,
Excitement and joy, forever in store!

Gently Speaking in Ripples

In the waves, fish gossip, quite absurd,
They chat about shells, and the odd sea bird.
A jellyfish floats, doing its dance,
Making silly faces, in a trance.

The crabs have meetings, under the sand,
Debating on lunch, a buffet so grand.
They wear tiny hats, like they're on parade,
Snapping their claws, in a goofy charade.

Seagulls are swoopers, with a knack for flair,
They swoop for a fry, pretending not to care.
Then they strut around, all puffed up with pride,
While the fishes below giggle, full of inside.

The tides joke with rocks, whispering glee,
As they peek at the shore, oh look, there's a bee!
And while the sun dips, turning skies bright,
The sea winks and waves, with sheer delight.

The Touch of Wave-drenched Memories

Once a sea turtle, slow and wise,
Said to a crab, with glaring eyes,
"Why rush to your meal, when sunsets glow?"
"Because I'm always late, and everyone knows!"

The dolphins play tag, all splashes and spins,
Teasing each other, with goofy grins.
They leap through the air, like they're on a show,
While the starfish below just giggle, and glow.

The flounders are flat, with a knack for disguise,
They lay on the ocean floor, much to our surprise.
While the rays glide by, saying "Catch me if you can!"
The flounders just laugh, that's part of their plan.

Eels give a fright, with a jolt and a squirm,
But really they're shy, if you touch their sweet worm.
As lids close with dusk on this comical theme,
The waves start to hum with a wink and a dream.

Ebbing Echoes of Day

Fish line up neatly, in front of the shore,
Practicing swims as they ask for an encore.
A whale drops in, like a plop from above,
Saying, "I too want to dance, show me some love!"

An octopus giggles, with colors that change,
Too shy to come out, thinking it's strange.
Yet it juggles some shells, much to our surprise,
With many slimy arms, it draws laughing eyes.

A boat floats on by, with a crew full of cheer,
Searchin' for treasure or maybe a beer.
But the real pearls lie where the sand meets the blue,
In laughter and pranks that belong to the crew.

The tide rolls away, with a splash and a sigh,
As the sun starts to set, painting the sky.
And the ocean hums softly, with joy in its sway,
In a world made of giggles, come play with the day.

When the Water Whispers

Driftwood confides in a starfish nearby,
"Why do you just sit there, and not even try?"
The starfish then chuckles, then rolls in a flair,
"I'm busy thinking thoughts of my next sunbath dare!"

A pelican swoops low, with a major blunder,
Missing his mouthful, oh what a wonder.
He shakes his big head, with a frown and a squawk,
While fish below chuckle, as they swim and gawk.

Seashells conspire, they gossip and tease,
About little crabs and their busy careers.
Fighting for food, with their aerial strikes,
While the seaweed curls, laughing, on its bikes.

As night brings the stars and the tide gives a yawn,
The water hums softly, until early dawn.
A lullaby dances, across the great swells,
In the heart of the ocean, where whimsy still dwells.

Harmonies of the Infinite Abyss

Bubbles rise with laughter's cheer,
Jellyfish dance, they seem so near.
Crabs do the cha-cha on the sand,
While seagulls squawk with a band.

Octopus plays a slick guitar,
Turtles groove, they're quite bizarre.
Fish form a conga line in blue,
Each splash is laughter, always new.

Starfish cheer on with silent glee,
Urchins giggle quietly.
Waves tickle toes on a sunny day,
Ocean antics come out to play.

Mermaids giggle with shells in tow,
Synchronized swimming, quite the show!
The waves, they laugh as they roll and crest,
In this watery world, we're truly blessed.

Tranquility Amongst the Waves

Paddle boats require balance and grace,
But water fights make a splashy race.
Seashells boast of tales they tell,
While sandy toes squish, oh so well!

Gulls swoop low with a wink and a dive,
Scaring sunbathers alive and jive.
Kids build castles, then watch them drown,
As waves giggle, they never frown.

Kites flutter high, seeking to roam,
While flip-flops fly like birds from home.
The sun sets low, the sky ignites,
With twinkling stars, oh what a sight!

Yet all around, the water's voice,
Makes us chuckle, we have no choice.
With each whitecap and joyful giggle,
In this beachy bliss, we dance and wiggle.

The Ocean's Gentle Caress

Whispers float on the briny breeze,
Starfish juggling with practiced ease.
Surfboards tipped, riders take their chance,
As dolphins leap in a playful dance.

Cranky old crabs claim their rock,
Complaining loud, they're quite the shock.
Mermaids debate which song to sing,
While sea cucumbers do their thing.

Seashells gossip about recent tides,
While seaweed sways, it never hides.
Clam shells clap with a rhythmic sound,
Echoes of joy in waves abound.

Salted hair and sun-kissed skin,
Every splash guarantees a grin.
The shoreline hums a giggling tune,
Where fun and laughter makes us swoon.

Shadows of Forgotten Whispers

Barnacles tap dance on the pier,
Seagulls chat, but we cannot hear.
Old buoys bob with a chuckle sound,
As forgotten ships turn around.

The wind tickles sails, they start to sway,
Each gust a joke in playful array.
Treasure maps lead to odd delight,
A rubber duck in pirate's sight.

Whales share secrets in bubbles blown,
While fish play hide and seek alone.
Lights shimmer as stars wink from above,
Each whispered laugh, a way to love.

As the tide rolls in and out with cheer,
Laughter echoes, oh so near.
In shadows of whispers, the fun lets flow,
In the arms of the water, we laugh and glow.

The Blue Embrace

The waves tickle toes, a playful tease,
Crabs in tuxedos dance with ease.
Seagulls squawk jokes in a squishy way,
While fish wear top hats, oh what a display!

The sun plays fetch with a bright, red ball,
Sandcastles crumble, they take a small fall.
A dog leaps high, catching bubbles mid-air,
While beach balls frolic without a care.

Flip-flops off, it's time for some fun,
We'll race the tides, oh, we'll never run!
And with a splash, our laughter fills the breeze,
As clams hide their smiles, behind sandy trees.

So gather 'round, let's sing loud and clear,
The ocean's our friend, let's cheer, let's cheer!
With a wink and a grin, the tide rolls away,
In this blue embrace, we all love to play.

Rhythm of the Shore

The waves do a jig, oh what a sight,
While seashells tap dance, feeling so light.
Crabs in a conga line wiggle and sway,
With jellyfish gliding, joining the play.

A dolphin pops up, does a flip in the air,
With seagulls above, they laugh without care.
The foam's like whipped cream on a cake by the tide,
As a starfish teaches a snail how to glide.

Sandcastles giggle, the sun sets in style,
While kids do their best to catch a big smile.
Tides bring us gossip from mermaids afar,
As crabs exchange tales at the edge of the bar.

The rhythm's contagious, we dance on the shore,
With sand in our shoes, who could ask for more?
Let's shimmy and shake till the moon takes a peek,
For in this wet world, it's laughter we seek.

Dances of the Distant Horizon

The gulls are the dancers, with feathers arranged,
While the waves practice twirls, all perfectly staged.
A whale's in the audience, nodding with glee,
As the tide bows down, whispering 'Follow me!'

Paddling penguins form a conga line,
While sea turtles groove, can't help but shine.
An octopus juggles, what a sight to behold,
Winking at squids, they're terribly bold.

The wind plays the piano, notes light as a kite,
With sand grains tapping, they're feeling just right.
A clownfish is laughing, wearing a grin,
As the reef joins the fun, let the party begin!

So far on the horizon, the sun gives a spin,
And the laughter grows louder, with every new win.
As the night joins the dance, with stars shining bright,
We'll sway to the rhythm until it's goodnight.

Nightfall's Soft Serenade

As stars peek out, the ocean's a charmer,
The moon pulls the waves in an elegant armor.
Crabs share secrets with the shadows they cast,
While night's gentle lullabies whisper at last.

The fish blush with laughter, under silvery light,
While glowing plankton put on a delight.
A dolphin croons softly, a lull in the tide,
While winking starfish hold hands, side by side.

With laughter and splashes, the night tries to peek,
As the sky paints a mural, unique and sleek.
The seaweed sways gently, a dancer's embrace,
And crickets join in with a soft, rhythmic grace.

So snuggle down close, let your worries all fade,
For the night hums a tune, a soft masquerade.
With dreams set adrift on the currents so free,
In this tranquil world, come dance with the sea.

Echoes in the Brine

Bubbles popped and fishy laughs,
A crab does dance while seagulls chaff.
Mermaids snicker, tails they swish,
Finding treasures, yearning for a fish.

Waves that giggle, splash with glee,
Octopuses hiding, can't you see?
With every swell, a silly tune,
A dolphin hums beneath the moon.

Shells that whisper, tales of yore,
A starfish smiles, but wants some more.
Jellyfish jiggle, what a sight,
In their jellies, they take flight!

Sand castles crumble, kids all cheer,
A seagull swoops, oh dear, oh dear!
Laughter caught in salty air,
In this realm of joy, we share.

Sighs of Distant Shores

Waves clap hands, what a surprise,
Clam and crab in a dance that flies.
Sunburnt surfers stumble and fall,
Seagulls chuckle, oh what a brawl!

The tide rolls in, a ticklish prank,
Fish wear hats, forming a flank.
"Tap dance with me," the dolphin beams,
Together we sway, lost in dreams.

Otters sliding on seaweed slides,
Pufferfish puffing, oh how they bide.
Gulls holding court, they squawk and jest,
Their jokes are terrible, still, they're the best!

Crabby complaints in a watery tone,
Clucky seagulls, not alone.
When the tide retreats, laughter swells,
Every grain of sand, a tale it tells.

Harmony of the Moonlit Waters

Under the stars, a whale does hum,
A fishy friend, where'd you come from?
Moonbeams giggle as they splash,
Shiny scales twinkle in a dash.

"Don't take my snack!" a sea turtle pleads,
As krill play tag amidst the weeds.
Horseshoe crabs wear funky shoes,
Strutting their stuff, they can't lose!

With every wave, a chuckle flows,
Caught in ripples, everything glows.
The sea, it chuckles with every dunk,
A playful world for all the funk.

Tides that tickle, kisses of foam,
Bubbles giggling, finding a home.
In the night, the ocean's cheer,
Echoes of laughter, oh so dear.

Tranquil Chants at Dusk

As daylight fades, the fish all sing,
While clams and crabs do their thing.
Mollusks gossip, sharing a grin,
"We'll dance like fools, let the fun begin!"

Stars will wink, the night is alive,
In tidal pools, the critters thrive.
Jellyfish float, bobbing with ease,
While scallops flutter in the breeze.

Waves, they whisper, tales of delight,
Puffins parade, what a silly sight!
Their beaks hold fish, laughing, they boast,
Under moonlit skies, they gather and toast.

Shores that shimmer in dusky light,
Laughter echoes, oh what a sight!
The ocean sighs, with joy it thrills,
In harmony, it captures our wills.

Tales of the Quiet Deep

Bubbles rise, fish dance with glee,
A clam's quirky tale spills endlessly.
Octopus juggling, a starfish on a quest,
In a world where the critters jest at their best.

A turtle in glasses, so wise yet so slow,
His jokes float like seaweed, a bizarre show.
Shrimp can't stop laughing, they're in quite a bind,
With a kraken named Larry who's one of a kind.

Seahorses prance in a lyrical spree,
Catching the rhythm, wild and free.
But watch for the crab with a claw just for fun,
He'll pinch you hard if you try to run!

So here's to the ocean, where humor's the swell,
In the realm of the deep, there's a cheerful swell.
Tales from the tide bring a grin big and bright,
As laughter floats gently into the night.

Celestial Harmony at Dusk

The moon takes a dip, a splash that's quite bold,
While fish throw a party, their scales turned to gold.
A crab strums a guitar, harmony near,
As jellyfish jiggle, floating without fear.

Dolphins in capes dive through the stars,
Making wishes on bubbles, dreaming of jars.
But watch for the seal, with a pun on the side,
He's prone to outsmart the whole ocean tide.

Whales hum a tune, quite off the beat,
Their song makes the walrus tap his big feet.
As starfish wink and wink, trying to bluff,
Even the plankton are giggling enough.

Under the twilight, with laughter so sweet,
The ocean's the stage, and life's quite a feat.
Embrace the silliness, let joys take a chance,
The cosmos rejoices in a curious dance.

Soft-Voiced Waters

In puddles abound, a frog wears a crown,
Croaking out jokes, he's the talk of the town.
With bubbles for laughs and waves for claps,
The seaweed's aflutter in giggly flaps.

A fish on a bicycle zooms past with flair,
While crabs throw confetti — oh, what a hair!
Seashells chime in, they can't hold a note,
But add to the chorus, they just rock the boat.

A dolphin's got hiccups, oh, what a sight,
He flips on the surface, the crowd pure delight.
Clownfish in makeup, they've put on a show,
In the watery world, there's laughter to grow.

So raise up a glass of sea-sparkling cheer,
Let the soft-voiced waters bring joy that's sincere.
In this playful domain where humor runs free,
Every splash is a giggle, just wait and see!

Reflections of the Secret Cove

In the hush of the cove, where giggles abound,
Mermaids throw parties, music's all around.
A sea turtle named Carl with a hat made of foam,
Claims he's the king, and this is his home.

Fish whisper secrets in colors so bright,
While crabs pull pranks under the soft moonlight.
A seagull just swoops, crashing his own show,
With a squawk that says, 'I'm the star of the flow!'

Whispers of waves tell tales that are odd,
Like sea cucumbers thinking they're gods.
As starry night drapes a blanket of fun,
The tide comes alive, the jokes have begun.

In the cove's gentle embrace, laughter flows free,
Where every ripple carries glee.
So dive into silliness, splash with delight,
In this secretive haven, the humor's just right!

Sonnet of the Undulating Waves

Waves waltz in rhythm, a comical dance,
Splashing in laughter, they take every chance.
With seagulls a-squawking, they join in the fun,
Two fish in tuxedos, both ready to run.

As surfboards glide by, the waves raise their brows,
"Who needs to surf? We can take our own bows!"
A crab pulls a prank with a pinch and a grin,
While a dolphin does flips, a sly wink in chin.

The tide rolls in whispers, tickling the sand,
With every quick ripple, they play hand in hand.
A jellyfish jokes, bouncing high with delight,
As sunbeams glow gently, they party all night.

Oh, the waves cackle on with their watery cheer,
The ocean's own giggles float far and quite near.
With joy in their bubbles, they never get sad,
Their shimmery laughter, the best fun they've had!

Chorus of the Coral Reefs

In the reef, a choir of colors so bright,
Fish wear top hats, a bizarre sight!
A starfish conducts with a wave of a limb,
While lobsters do tango, their moves are quite grim.

The sea crawlers croon in spectacular tune,
A clownfish is laughing beneath the full moon.
Coral groans gently, a joke on its face,
As an octopus juggles, the crowd sings in grace.

With bubbles and giggles, they frolic and play,
Each snicker and chortle, the highlights of day.
The parrotfish chuckles, in polka dot threads,
While anemones sway, sharing tales in their beds.

So join in the humor, the oceanic jest,
Where every fish giggles, and all are impressed.
A carnival under, where laughter's the theme,
In the underwater choir, we all share a dream!

Memories Written in Foam

Foamy footprints linger on the soft shore,
Wave compliments making the sands ask for more.
Each bubble a giggle that echoes the past,
A tale of the tide that forever will last.

A starfish recalls its wild night in the sea,
When crabs played charades like a grand jubilee.
The seaweed laughed hard, doing flips in the breeze,
As fish wore their costumes, they swam with such ease.

Seagulls exchanging their gossip on high,
"Did you see the clam dance? It nearly could fly!"
The waves keep on chuckling, never in fright,
As they tickle the edges, both day and night.

So when waves whisper softly to the sand,
Remember their stories, together they stand.
In frothy embraces of fun and delight,
The ocean keeps secrets, both silly and bright!

Tales from a Sailor's Rest

In the tavern's corner, a sailor recounts,
A mermaid, quite cheeky, and her fish friends' flounce.
With tales of grand sea battles, he sways with a grin,
While a parrot squawks loudly, "Let the fun begin!"

The sailor spills stories of storms gone awry,
How a whale tried to dance, but flopped on the sly.
A sea urchin pondered, "What's the meaning of life?"
While barnacles giggled at a crab's silly strife.

The wind sings a jig as his mug fills with cheer,
And laughter erupts, echoing far and near.
With each dramatic wave, and tall tale of lore,
The ocean's own mischief is hard to ignore.

So raise up your glasses, toast to the brine,
For tales of the sea are truly divine.
In a boat of pure whimsy, float laughter and song,
Where sailors and fish both know they belong!

The Ballad of the Brine

Bubbles burble with glee,
Fish wearing hats, oh so free!
Crabs do the cha-cha by the rocks,
While seagulls squawk in silly flocks.

Turtles tango, taking it slow,
Starfish twirl in a dazzling show!
An octopus winks with eight little eyes,
Making all the sea creatures laugh with surprise.

Jellyfish bounce like they're on a spree,
Riding the currents, oh what a spree!
Clams clap together in rhythmic delight,
While the sun sets the ocean's stage alight.

With every wave, a chuckle or two,
The briny blues sing their own tune,
Where laughter ripples beneath the foam,
In this underwater, jovial home.

Above and Below the Surface

Seagulls giggle as they dive-bomb,
Splashing the fish, who squawk in alarm,
The kelp sways like it's on a dance floor,
While the waves roll in with a thunderous roar.

Beneath the blue, there's quite a rave,
A dolphin makes moves that surely amaze,
Bubble parties with mermaids invite,
As seaweed twirls, it's quite the sight!

A crab in a tux, he's ready to date,
But the octopus steals the show, it's fate,
With eight arms waving, he makes them swoon,
Like he's grooving to a catchy tune.

Above, the sun sets, painting the scene,
While below, it's a mishmash of green,
In this world where laughter prevails,
Even the starfish tell silly tales!

Caresses in Waveform

The ocean giggles, tickling toes,
As gentle waves sway to and fro,
A crab makes jokes about his old shell,
While clams retort, "That's not how we sell!"

Barnacles gossip on the side of the rocks,
They chatter all day, just like a box,
"Did you hear what the sea cucumber said?
He claims he's tougher than any old thread!"

A sea turtle in shades swims by with style,
"Catch me if you can," he shouts with a smile,
Meanwhile, a dolphin holds a karaoke night,
And all the fish join in, singing with plight.

Waves roll in, bringing tales from afar,
Of pirate ships and a lost candy jar,
In the sea's embrace, the laughter is loud,
Every splash creates a giggling crowd.

Resonance of the Blue Abyss

In the deep blue, where giggles flow,
There's an anchovy who steals the show,
With a tiny top hat and a flair for fun,
He leads the fish in a wild run.

A clam in a conch thinks he's all that,
But the fish just roll their eyes, "What a brat!"
The seaweed sways, gets caught in the fray,
As waves burst forth, sending laughter their way.

Bubbles rise like balloons in a fair,
While a starfish juggles, trying to dare,
The gulls laugh above, munching on fries,
As the sun kisses down with twinkling eyes.

Echoes of joy in the watery dome,
Where every splash feels just like home,
The resonance of mirth in the ocean's embrace,
Turns the blue abyss into a playful space.

Notes of Memory in Tidal Pools

In a tidal pool, a crab wore a hat,
Sipping seaweed tea, imagine that!
Starfish twirled, in dancing delight,
The ocean chuckled, oh what a sight!

A drifty fish said, "I've lost my shoe!"
Tiny clams giggled, said, "We've lost two!"
With sea cucumbers, they played a game,
Making memories that never feel lame.

An octopus juggled pearls with a grin,
While blushing anemones joined in the spin.
The tide rolled in, they laughed and swayed,
In this watery world, worries decayed.

When waves roll out, they all just freeze,
As seagulls debate, who's the best tease.
Tidal pools giggle, their secrets unfold,
In salty embraces, their stories are told.

Lanterns of the Deep

In the deep blue, fish wear bright hats,
Dancing under bubbles, in fancy flats.
Jellyfish bob, with a twinkle of light,
Swaying in rhythms, oh what a sight!

Crabs play chess on a deck made of sea,
Arguing loudly, as crabs tend to be.
A whale nearby hums a tune, so grand,
Together they sway, a light-hearted band.

Turtles bring snacks from the deep ocean floor,
Sharing their treats, what a seafood store!
The lantern fish giggle, with beams aglow,
In a festival of lights, putting on a show.

As currents swish, they twirl with ease,
While a cheerful grouper begs for a tease.
In this underwater gala, laughter prevails,
With melodious bubbles, their joy never fails.

Whispers of Maritime Tales

At the docks, a gull spins tales of the fry,
While fish in the nets roll their eyes, oh my!
A shark tells a story of treasure once found,
But the salmon just giggles, shaking, unbound.

The lighthouse keeper shares jokes with the tide,
While dolphins perform, wearing smiles wide.
Waves elevate laughter, a chorus of fun,
As the sun dips down and the sea starts to run.

With barnacles grinning on boats drifting by,
And a clam with a monocle, oh me, oh my!
They reminisce fondly of waves they have crossed,
In a maritime debate, no one feels lost.

So gather your memories and drift into dreams,
Where nautical fables twist into teams.
In every wave, let a story accrue,
In the whispers of water, life starts anew.

Silhouettes by the Shore

By the shore, silhouettes dance in the sand,
As crabs do the cha-cha, how silly they stand!
Children giggle as seagulls swoop low,
While waves keep the rhythm, a bright ebb and flow.

A beach ball bounces, doing flips with glee,
As shells have a party, a jubilee spree.
The tide ticks life, like a whimsical clock,
And sea turtles join in with a quirky rock!

Pails full of laughter spill over the edge,
With sandcastles topped by a seaweedy hedge.
Fish peek and splash just to join in the fun,
And the sun shines down—oh, what a run!

So come to the coast where the shadows play,
With seaside whispers to brighten your day.
In every grain of sand, there's a tale to unfold,
Where humor and waves weave stories retold.

The Palette of Nautical Calm

Underneath the waves, fish dance all day,
One tries to juggle, but swims away.
Seagulls squawk tunes, quite off the beat,
Waves join in, tapping their sandy feet.

Shells hold gossip, secrets they share,
A crab in a tux, who claims he's a heir.
Colors of coral, a painter's delight,
But the jellyfish do their own thing at night.

A pirate's hat floats, lost in the fray,
Complains it misses its captain's toupee.
Turtles wear shades as they lounge on the shore,
While the dolphins giggle, still wanting more.

So raise a toast with a seaweed twist,
To the quirky creatures we surely missed.
With laughter and bubbles, we float on our song,
In the whimsical world where we all belong.

Songs of Forgotten Mariner Souls

Forgotten sailors sing in the breeze,
Their tales of mishaps, lost treasure, and cheese.
They charted the stars, but bumped into lamps,
Navigating waters with spontaneous camps.

Their courage was great, but their sense was quite bad,
They wrestled with krakens, oh my, how they'd rad!
With parrot companions, they'd laugh and they'd bow,
As a fish on the line would give them a wow.

Now they haunt the shores with a wink and a grin,
"Arrr" with a chuckle, for all they could spin.
A mermaid named Sally, with a beard made of foam,
Swims past the sailors, calling each one home.

So raise your glass high for a toast to the lost,
To the mariner souls who paid quite the cost.
With their silly old stories of stormy delight,
They've turned every wrong into a glorious right.

Flowing Verses of the Water's Edge

Down at the river where the ducks do the waltz,
A fish claims he's swimming with crustacean pals.
The rocks are all chatting, gossiping fast,
"Did you see that fish? He was quite the outcast!"

A boat comes floating, with snacks piled high,
While a frog in a crown aims to catch the eye.
He croaks out a sonnet, all melodious cheer,
While turtles nearby nod, "Let's give him a beer!"

The wavy reflections, they poke fun at the sun,
Trying to outshine, oh what a silly run!
Clouds in confusion, drifting in styles,
As they overheard fish telling laughable trials.

At dusk near the shores, laughter carries on,
With crickets as choruses, they sing 'til the dawn.
In this flowing world, under skies all aglow,
Each ripple a chuckle in the show of the show.

A Tryst with Serenity

A dapper old otter in boots made of lace,
Swings by to chat, with a grin on his face.
"Have you seen the sea cows with party-themed hats?
They're dancing tonight with the fancy sea rats!"

The waves giggle back as they lap at the shore,
Sharing the whispers of tales and folklore.
A crab tells a joke that makes everyone snicker,
While the starfish gather for martinis, much quicker!

Seashells are singing, in chorus divine,
While turtles in bowties join in with a line.
"Chill out with your worries, let laughter prevail,
Even sea monsters can't resist this good tale!"

So here's to the waters, so funny and free,
Where calmness meets giggles, oh so carefree!
With sparkles and sunshine that shimmer and sway,
Join in the tryst where we laugh all day.

Cadences of Water's Embrace

Waves dance like they wear fancy shoes,
Splashing around with playful hues.
Fish hold meetings under the waves,
Arguing over the best kelp caves.

Seagulls sing with a raucous tune,
While crabs play tag beneath the moon.
Turtles glide in their slow-motion race,
All while jellyfish float with grace.

Barnacles gossip on the old, wet rocks,
Whispering secrets like cheeky clocks.
Saltwater tickles every fishy face,
Making them giggle in their wet embrace.

The tides come in with a playful shove,
As if they're trying to share their love.
In this watery world, fun's never done,
We all laugh under the bright sun.

The Silent Call of the Ocean

Bubbles rise like messages in a bottle,
Fish joke and laugh, it's never a coddle.
Seaweed sways, dancing all around,
While crabs click-clack without making a sound.

Waves whisper tales of pirates past,
But it's the dolphins who run super fast.
They leap like they've got something to prove,
Making the surf feel like a lively groove.

Anemones wiggle, tickling the toes,
Of those who wander where the tide flows.
Starfish play hide-and-seek on the shore,
Laughing at humans who just want more.

A clam's surprised face as it gets a peep,
At silly octopuses, giggling in sleep.
This watery realm is a merry delight,
Where laughter echoes through the moonlit night.

Dreams Amidst the Briny Depths

Down below, where the bubbles jest,
Creatures convene for a daily fest.
Octopuses wear hats made of coral,
Dancing beneath the sea's grand portal.

Crabs choose partners with a sideways glide,
Claiming their spots like they're full of pride.
The flounders play poker, all hidden and sly,
While eels debate who will win the pie.

A whale's deep laugh echoes through the foam,
Causing fish to scatter, seeking their home.
Sea cucumbers chill, acting so aloof,
But whisper sweet secrets under the roof.

With each little wave, a chuckle is shared,
As the bright reef folks nibble and dared.
In briny dreams where most creatures play,
Laughter bubbles forth every single day.

Lull of the Horizon

As the sun dips down in a splash of gold,
Fish tell stories that never get old.
Crabs with top hats march in a line,
While sea stars gossip over a glass of brine.

Blowfish puff up just for a laugh,
Teasing the sharks who prefer their 'half.'
Coral castles stand, regal and bright,
Hosting sea parties in the deep of night.

A dolphin's flick is a humorous dance,
Attracting the crowd with their silly prance.
And two friendly whales share a warm joke,
As they moo-laugh through a bubble smoke.

The horizons are home to a thousand odd sights,
Where laughter lives on sea's gentle flights.
So here's to the joy that the waves bring along,
In the quiet embrace of the sea's soft song.

www.ingramcontent.com/pod-product-compliance
Lightning Source LLC
Chambersburg PA
CBHW060145230426
43661CB00003B/575